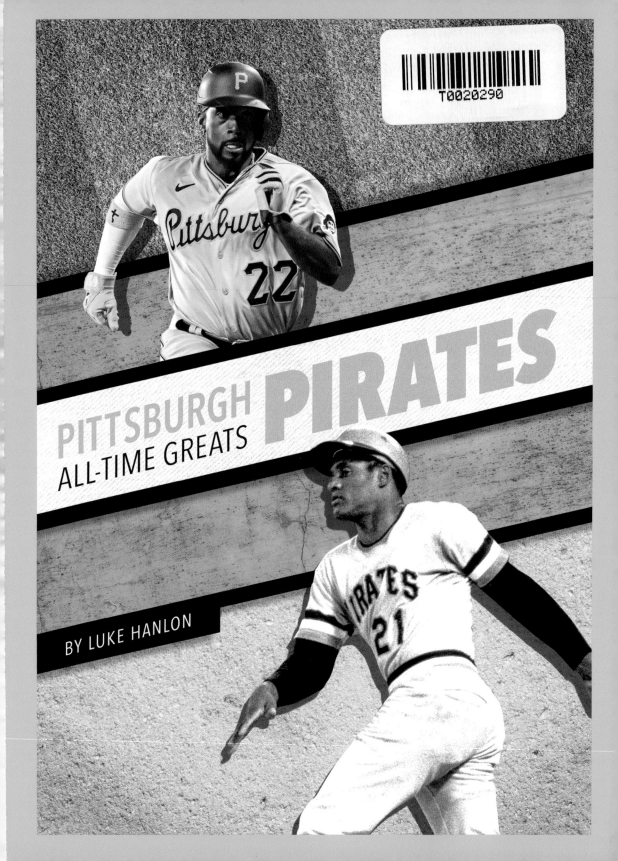

PITTSBURGH PIRATES

ALL-TIME GREATS

BY LUKE HANLON

Book design by Jake Slavik
Cover design by Jake Slavik

Photographs ©: Rick Ulreich/Icon Sportswire/AP Images, cover (top), 1 (top); Rusty Kennedy/AP Images, cover (bottom), 1 (bottom); Mark Rucker/Transcendental Graphics/Getty Images Sport/Getty Images, 4, 8; AP Images, 7, 13; Bettmann/Getty Images, 10; Focus On Sport/Getty Images Sport/Getty Images, 15; Rich Pilling/Getty Images Sport/Getty Images, 16; George Gojkovich/Getty Images Sport/Getty Images, 18; Ron Vesely/MLB Photos/Getty Images Sport/Getty Images, 21

Press Box Books, an imprint of Press Room Editions.

ISBN
978-1-63494-800-5 (library bound)
978-1-63494-820-3 (paperback)
978-1-63494-858-6 (epub)
978-1-63494-840-1 (hosted ebook)

Library of Congress Control Number: 2023910373

Distributed by North Star Editions, Inc.
2297 Waters Drive
Mendota Heights, MN 55120
www.northstareditions.com

Printed in the United States of America
012024

ABOUT THE AUTHOR

Luke Hanlon is a sportswriter and editor based in Minneapolis.

TABLE OF CONTENTS

WAGNER

CHAPTER 1
EARLY PIRATES

The Pittsburgh Pirates had already existed for 21 years when the first World Series took place in 1903. Representing the National League (NL), Pittsburgh made it to that World Series thanks in large part to **Honus Wagner**. A rival manager once described Wagner as the "nearest thing to a perfect player."

The shortstop was an excellent fielder. But where Wagner truly frightened opponents was at the plate. In 18 seasons with the Pirates, Wagner led the NL in batting average a record eight times. Wagner finished his career with more than 600 doubles and 250 triples.

Fred Clarke was the Pirates manager in 1903. He was also the team's left fielder. Like Wagner, Clarke was masterful at the plate. The Boston Americans beat the Pirates in the 1903 World Series. But Clarke led the Pirates back in 1909. Wagner and Clarke combined for 12 hits and 13 runs batted in (RBIs) in that series. The Pirates beat the Detroit Tigers in seven games.

Outfielder **Max Carey** played in Pittsburgh for 17 seasons. The speedy baserunner led the NL in stolen bases in 10 different seasons with the Pirates. **Pie Traynor** was known as the

MILLION-DOLLAR CARD

There were 206 Honus Wagner T206 baseball cards made between 1909 and 1911. Over time, the rare card has become incredibly valuable. The T206 has been sold for more than $1 million multiple times. In 2022, one of the cards sold for $7.25 million.

TRAYNOR
20

best third baseman in the league for years. His combination of power and speed helped him hit triples with ease. The duo of Carey and Traynor led the Pirates back to the World Series in 1925. They combined for 20 hits and helped the Pirates beat the Washington Senators in seven games.

WANER
11

8

Paul Waner made his Major League Baseball (MLB) debut the next season. The right fielder led the NL with 22 triples as a rookie. He was even better in 1927. Waner led the league in hits, triples, RBIs, and batting average. Waner's impressive total earned him the NL Most Valuable Player (MVP) Award.

Shortstop **Arky Vaughan** won the NL batting title by hitting .385 in 1935. That year he made his second straight All-Star Game. Vaughan had played in five more by the time he left the Pirates after the 1941 season. He also hit better than .300 in each of his 10 seasons with Pittsburgh.

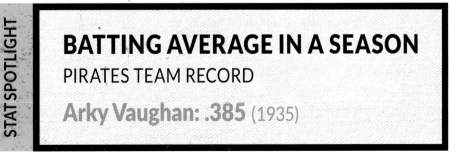

STAT SPOTLIGHT

BATTING AVERAGE IN A SEASON
PIRATES TEAM RECORD
Arky Vaughan: .385 (1935)

KINER
4

CHAPTER 2
PRIDE OF PITTSBURGH

After a couple down years, the Pirates had become one of MLB's finest teams once again by the 1950s. **Ralph Kiner** was an instant star after his debut in 1946. Kiner had a powerful swing. He used it to smack home runs into what became known as "Kiner's Korner" in Forbes Field.

The Pirates continued to stack up talent. **Vern Law** debuted in 1950. In 1960, Law exploded. The righty threw a league-high 18 complete games. **Bob Friend** earned the nickname "Warrior" after joining in 1951. He never spent a day on the injured list in

15 seasons with the Pirates. Shortstop **Dick Groat** arrived in 1952. Like Law, he was at his best in 1960. Groat won the NL batting title that year, hitting .325.

Two of Pittsburgh's biggest stars came to town in the mid-1950s. **Roberto Clemente** debuted in 1955. **Bill Mazeroski** joined the team a year later. By 1960, the Pirates were dominating. Law earned the MLB Cy Young Award that season. This award was given to the best pitcher in the majors each year. Later, the rule was changed so the best pitcher in each league earned one. Meanwhile, Groat was the

CAREER STRIKEOUTS
PIRATES TEAM RECORD
Bob Friend: 1,682

MAZEROSKI
9

NL MVP in 1960. The Pirates made it to the World Series that year and faced the New York Yankees. It came down to the wire.

In Game 7, the teams were tied 9–9 in the bottom of the ninth. Mazeroski led off the inning. The second baseman was known mostly for his great defense. But his clutch walk-off home run won the World Series for Pittsburgh.

After a title-winning 1960 season, Clemente's stardom kept the Pirates rolling. In 1961, he won the first of four career NL batting titles. He also won his first Gold Glove that year. This award is given to the best fielder at each position. Clemente won 12 straight. His best hitting year came in 1966. His 29 home runs and 119 RBIs were both career highs. And Clemente was the NL MVP that season.

The Pirates made it back to the World Series in 1971. Clemente stole

GONE TOO SOON

Roberto Clemente recorded his 3,000th hit on September 30, 1972. He was the 11th player in MLB history to reach that total. And he was the first Latino player to do it. Unfortunately, that ended up being his last regular-season hit. On December 31, 1972, Clemente was on a flight to Nicaragua to help provide relief after an earthquake. The plane crashed in the ocean, killing everyone on board.

CLEMENTE
21

the show. He shelled the Baltimore Orioles
pitchers, hitting .414. Clemente won the World
Series MVP Award for his efforts, as Pittsburgh
came away with another title in seven games.

STARGELL
8

CHAPTER 3
FAMILY AND FUTURE

Willie Stargell also helped the Pirates in their 1971 World Series season. The star left fielder led the NL with 48 home runs that year. Stargell led the league again in 1973. His 119 RBIs topped the NL as well.

Stargell continued to star for the Pirates throughout the 1970s. He was joined by slugger **Dave Parker**. The right fielder was

STAT SPOTLIGHT

CAREER HOME RUNS
PIRATES TEAM RECORD
Willie Stargell: 475

CANDELARIA 45

the 1978 NL MVP after hitting .334 with 117 RBIs. On the mound, lefty **John Candelaria** went from star prospect to 20-game winner in 1977. Meanwhile, reliever **Kent Tekulve** recorded 31 saves in both 1978 and 1979. This core helped the Pirates reach the 1979 World Series.

However, the series didn't start how Pittsburgh wanted. After four games, the Orioles led three games to one. But then

Pittsburgh's pitching took over. Candelaria, Tekulve, and the rest of the Pittsburgh pitching staff allowed only one run combined in Games 5 and 6. Pittsburgh rallied, and the two teams found themselves in a winner-take-all Game 7.

That was when Stargell took over. "Pops" went 4-for-5 at the plate, including a two-run homer in the sixth inning. This gave Pittsburgh a 2–1 lead. The team held on to win the championship. At 39 years old, Stargell was unstoppable in 1979. He was the NL MVP

WE ARE FAMILY

In 1979, "We Are Family" by Sister Sledge became an important song in Pittsburgh. A Pirates game was delayed due to rain. The song played throughout Three Rivers Stadium. Willie Stargell got staff to display "We Are Family" on the scoreboard as the team's theme song. The Pirates came back after trailing 8–5 in the ninth inning of that game. The song then became an inspiration for the rest of the season.

that season. He also won the MVP of the NL Championship Series (NLCS) and the World Series. No player had ever won all three in the same season.

Barry Bonds joined the Pirates in 1986. His elite athleticism eventually made him one of the game's best players. His speed made him a great base stealer and defender. His power made him a threat at the plate. Bonds won both the 1990 and 1992 NL MVP Awards while with Pittsburgh.

It took many years to find another star like Bonds. But **Andrew McCutchen** fit the bill after arriving in 2009. By 2013, he was the NL MVP. Like Bonds, McCutchen had a combination of speed and power. "Cutch" hit 203 homers and stole 171 bases in nine years with Pittsburgh. He left Pittsburgh in 2018, but

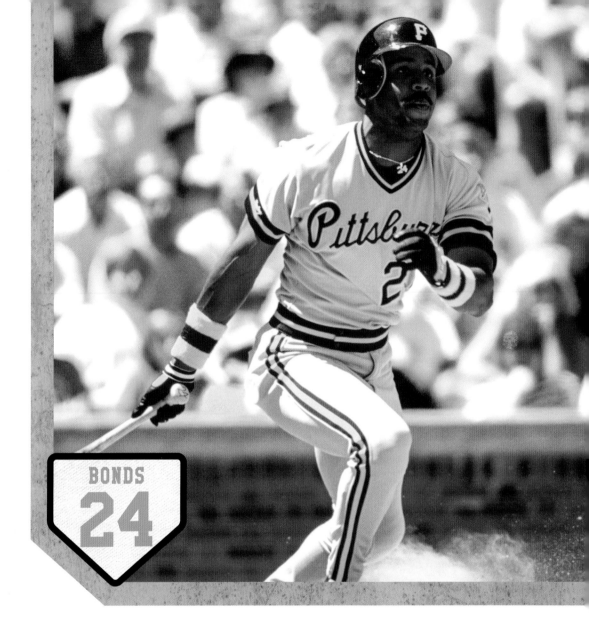

BONDS
24

McCutchen's return in 2023 gave Pirates fans hope they would see more playoff success in the near future.

TIMELINE

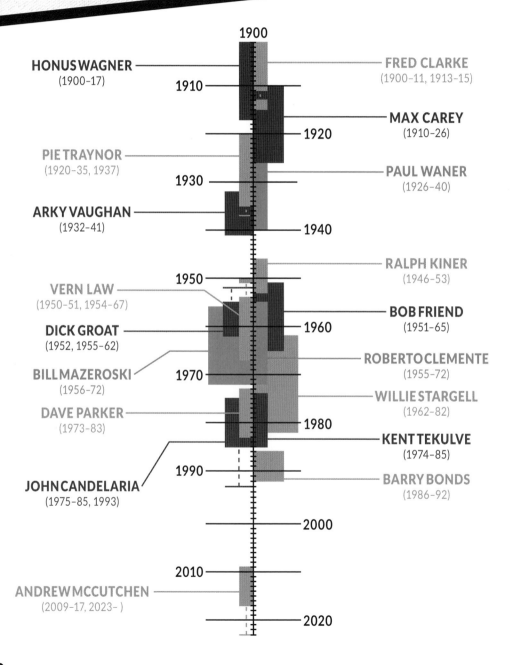

1900

HONUS WAGNER
(1900–17)

1910

MAX CAREY
(1910–26)

1920

PIE TRAYNOR
(1920–35, 1937)

PAUL WANER
(1926–40)

1930

ARKY VAUGHAN
(1932–41)

1940

RALPH KINER
(1946–53)

1950

VERN LAW
(1950–51, 1954–67)

BOB FRIEND
(1951–65)

DICK GROAT
(1952, 1955–62)

1960

BILL MAZEROSKI
(1956–72)

ROBERTO CLEMENTE
(1955–72)

1970

WILLIE STARGELL
(1962–82)

DAVE PARKER
(1973–83)

1980

KENT TEKULVE
(1974–85)

1990

JOHN CANDELARIA
(1975–85, 1993)

BARRY BONDS
(1986–92)

2000

2010

ANDREW MCCUTCHEN
(2009–17, 2023–)

2020

22

PITTSBURGH PIRATES

Team history: Pittsburgh Alleghenys (1882-90), Pittsburgh Pirates (1891-)

World Series titles: 5 (1909, 1925, 1960, 1971, 1979)*

Key managers:

Fred Clarke (1900-15)

    1,422-969 (.595), 1 World Series title

Danny Murtaugh (1957-64, 1967, 1970-71, 1973-76)

    1,115-950 (.540), 2 World Series titles

Chuck Tanner (1977-85)

    711-685 (.509), 1 World Series title

MORE INFORMATION

To learn more about the Pittsburgh Pirates, go to **pressboxbooks.com/AllAccess**.

These links are routinely monitored and updated to provide the most current information available.

*through 2022

GLOSSARY

clutch
Having to do with a difficult situation when the outcome of the game is in question.

complete game
When one pitcher throws every inning in a single game.

debut
First appearance.

elite
The best of the best.

prospect
A player that people expect to do well at a higher level.

rookie
A first-year player.

save
When a pitcher finishes a game where their team is winning by three runs or fewer.

walk-off
A play that ends the game.

INDEX